Coping with Change

HONOR HEAD

CRABTREE
PUBLISHING COMPANY
WWW.CRABTREEBOOKS.COM

CRABTREE
PUBLISHING COMPANY
WWW.CRABTREEBOOKS.COM

Published in Canada
Crabtree Publishing
616 Welland Ave.
St. Catharines, Ontario
L2M 5V6

Published in the United States
Crabtree Publishing
347 Fifth Avenue
Suite 1402–145
New York, NY 10016

Published in 2021 by Crabtree Publishing Company

First published in Great Britain in 2020
by The Watts Publishing Group
Copyright © The Watts Publishing Group, 2020

Author: Honor Head

Editorial director: Kathy Middleton

Editors: Amy Pimperton, Ellen Rodger

Proofreader: Melissa Boyce

Designers: Peter Scoulding and Cathryn Gilbert

Cover design: Peter Scoulding

Production coordinator
  and Prepress technician: Tammy McGarr

Print coordinator: Katherine Berti

Consultant: Clare Arnold, psychotherapist and child and adolescent mental health services professional

Printed in the U.S.A./012021/CG20201102

Picture credits
Shutterstock: Robert Adamec 14br; Andrew Astbury 5c; Mila Atkovska 21c; Arne von Brill Photo 29t; Orhan Cam 14l; Cat'chy 28l; Roger Clark ARPS 18; coolcat 5t, 30c; Coryn 7b; Delbars 10; Gorkem Demir 28cr; S Derevianko 13c; Dezy 25r, 26; Edgar Drieman 16; Emka74 27c, 32; Frank Fichtmuelle 22b; Nick Fox 19b; Arturo de Frias front cover, 1; Kev Gregory 15b; Anton Gvozdikov 21t; Hyserb 9cr; Annan Kaewhammul 11tl; Daniel Kay 5b; Grigorita Ko 2, 8, 17b, 24t; Holly Kuchera 13b; Viacheslav Maksimov 7t; Meirion Matthias 19c; Katho Menden 11bl; Maggy Meyer 9bl; Jeroen Mikkers 29b; Dave Montreuil 12; Ivanova N 21b; Nagel Photography 7c, 30t; NaturesMomentsuk 9tl; Orientgold 11cr; PCHT 19t; Jonathan Pledger 15t; Ondrej Prosicky 22t, 23r, 27b; David Rasmus 13t; Reptiles4all 17c; Schubbel 17t; Ajar Setiadi 23cl, 30b; S J Travel 4; Sergey Uryadnikov 25l; Colin Robert Varndell 27t; V-yan 24b; Asaf Wiesman 20; Phanuwat Yoksiri 6.

Library and Achives Canada Cataloguing in Publication

Title: Coping with change / Honor Head.
Names: Head, Honor, author.
Description: Series statement: Building resilience | Includes index.
Identifiers: Canadiana (print) 2020035678X | Canadiana (ebook) 20200356917
  ISBN 9781427128201 (hardcover) |
  ISBN 9781427128249 (softcover) |
  ISBN 9781427128287 (HTML)
Subjects: LCSH: Change (Psychology)—Juvenile literature. | LCSH: Resilience (Personality trait) in children—Juvenile literature.
Classification: LCC BF637.C4 H43 2021 | DDC j158.1—dc23

Library of Congress Cataloging-in-Publication Data

Names: Head, Honor, author.
Title: Coping with change / Honor Head.
Description: New York : Crabtree Publishing Company, 2021. |
  Series: Building resilience | Includes index.
Identifiers: LCCN 2020045187 (print) | LCCN 2020045188 (ebook) |
  ISBN 9781427128201 (hardcover) |
  ISBN 9781427128249 (paperback) |
  ISBN 9781427128287 (ebook)
Subjects: LCSH: Change (Psychology)--Juvenile literature. |
  Resilience (Personality trait) in children--Juvenile literature.
Classification: LCC BF637.C4 H423 2021 (print) | LCC BF637.C4 (ebook) |
  DDC 158.1--dc23
LC record available at https://lccn.loc.gov/2020045187
LC ebook record available at https://lccn.loc.gov/2020045188

Contents

Everyone faces challenging times in their life. This book will help you to develop the resilience skills you need to cope with difficult situations in all areas of life.

What does it mean to build resilience?

When we build resilience we can cope better with things, such as being bullied or losing a friend. Building resilience means we accept that times are difficult now, but that we can and will get back to enjoying life. Learning how to build resilience is a valuable life skill.

What is a trusted adult?

A trusted adult is anyone that you trust and who makes you feel safe. It can be a parent or caregiver, a relative, or a teacher. If you have no one you can to talk to, phone a helpline (see page 32).

Coping with change

Most people do the same things every day. They get up, get ready for school, see friends, eat dinner, watch TV, read, and go to bed.

Doing the same things every day can make people feel safe and in control.

Life is a series of changes. Some changes will be big, such as going to a new school or moving to a new home. Other changes will be small, such as eating something new.

It is important that we learn how to cope with change. Most changes are fun and exciting. But some changes can seem big and scary. Some changes will be difficult and we might not want to make them.

It is easier to cope with the uncertainty of change if you build your resilience. Resilience is the ability to bounce back from change.

Dealing with disappointment

Sudden change can be upsetting. If you are looking forward to a picnic and it starts pouring rain so you cannot go, you may feel **disappointed**.

Making last-minute changes to our plans can make us angry and upset.

There is nothing wrong with feeling disappointed, angry, sad, or upset. Sometimes you have to accept that there is nothing you can do about a situation.

Sometimes you can turn a bad thing into a good thing by being **positive**. If you cannot go on a picnic, there might be something else you can do that is just as much fun.

Being creative can help you deal with disappointment. Maybe you can play your favorite game or dress up in funny costumes. You could sit somewhere cozy and read, or tell stories while eating snacks.

Why change is good

Looking forward to change and not being scared of it is very good for us. It means we are more likely to try new things. Change can make life interesting and fun.

Trying new things means that you will meet new people.

By trying new things we learn that sometimes we fail, and that failure is not always a bad thing. Failing helps us not to be scared of doing something wrong. It gives us a chance to try again and get it right.

As we try new things we get a better idea of what we really enjoy doing and learning. Unless you try something new, how do you know if you will like it or not?

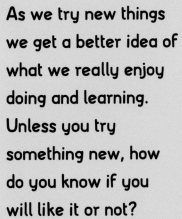

Trying new things builds up our **self-confidence** and makes us feel brave. It can help us bounce back from change.

Change your routine

A routine can make you feel confident.

Doing the same things in the same way every day makes us feel safe and **secure**. We know how to behave and we know what is going to happen. This is called a **routine**.

When you do the same things every day in the same way, your brain and body get used to it. When you change your routine, your brain has to think in a different way. This is good for your brain.

There are many ways to change your routine. You can get dressed in a different order. You can wear a different color, play different games, or change your room around.

Talk to your family about fun ways you can make everyday changes. A change of routine will be great for everyone.

Moving to a new home

Moving from one place to another can be stressful. You may be comfortable in your neighborhood or afraid of going to a new school. **Reframing** a move can help. Thinking about the people you will meet and the new places you will explore can help you feel better about a move.

Moving to a new home can be an exciting adventure.

Talk to your family if you feel **anxious** and upset about a move. It can help to visit your new home before you move. Then you can see what your new neighborhood is like and imagine doing fun things.

Be positive. Try to think of the move as a chance to try new things.

Photograph or draw the places you like where you live now, such as your school or park. Keep them in a memory book. Remember how happy you were at these places. In time, you can be just as happy in your new home.

New brother or sister

Having a new baby in the house is great. It can also be hard because the adults might not have as much time to spend with you. Babies need a lot of care. You may feel happy or upset when a new baby arrives. You may even feel both **emotions**.

A new baby changes the routine and this can be upsetting. Adults can help you feel you are part of the change.

It is OK to feel **jealous** and hurt when a new baby arrives. Talking about how you feel will help you bounce back to feeling like your old self.

Remember that however it seems, your family still loves you. Now you will have a brother or sister to love you, and someone new for you to love.

Being a big brother or sister is exciting, because they need you to help them grow up!

New stepsisters and stepbrothers could mean new friends for you.

Stepsisters and stepbrothers

Having a new family, such as stepsisters or stepbrothers, is a big change in your life. This change may make you feel scared or angry. It is easy to make our minds up about people without getting to know them first. Take a deep breath and try and get to know these new people in your life.

If you feel angry that you have to share your space with new people, you might say and do mean things. Instead of being mean, try to remember that the other person may also feel hurt and angry.

Get to know your new stepsisters and stepbrothers. Be kind and friendly to them. They probably feel a little scared as well.

Think of things to do together. Explore the local park or museum. Bake a cake, make a pizza, or have a family movie night.

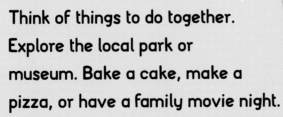

New stepparent

Having a new stepparent in your life does not mean that they have replaced your mom or dad. But you do need to learn to bounce back if this makes you feel sad or angry. Build resilience by remembering that now you have another parent who will love you and care for you.

Get to know your new stepparent and give them a chance to be friendly.

Talk to your family about how you feel about having a stepparent. It is very brave to be honest and to let others know what you are feeling. Sharing your feelings will help you feel better.

A good way to start talking is to draw a picture of how you feel. Sometimes it is easier to talk sitting side-by-side and not face-to-face.

Most adults will only want to look after you and care for you. But sometimes adults can say and do things that hurt you. If this happens, talk to someone you trust or phone a helpline.

Two homes

Often when parents separate, people have two homes. Visiting each parent in their own home means a big change in your routine. It can also make you feel upset and angry that your parents don't live together.

Having two homes can be confusing, but it could also be twice as much fun.

Talk to both of your parents about how you feel. Ask them to make a plan for which home you will be at when, and for how long, so you know what is happening.

Keep some of your favorite things at each home. These could be a favorite toy, a mug, or pajamas.

Ask if you can help choose the furnishings for your other bedroom. You could choose the curtains or blinds, a rug, night-light, or bedsheets.

Friends moving away

People move away for all sorts of reasons. Maybe it is to be closer to other family members or for work. A good friend moving away can make you feel lonely or unhappy. Sometimes life feels unfair.

When a friend moves away it will be difficult for both of you.

Both you and your friend will be sad when your friend moves away. Your friend will have to deal with all the changes as well. Talk with your friend about how you both feel about the move.

By sharing your feelings, you can help each other feel less scared about the move. Helping others makes us feel good and this helps us to bounce back.

If you feel cranky or angry, dance to your favorite music. Try letting it out by punching your pillow. Feel your emotions instead of holding them in.

23

keeping in touch

Before your friend moves, do something fun and creative together. By building happy memories and being positive, you can bounce back. This makes it easier to deal with difficult changes.

Have fun planning something special to do together.

Make a plan to keep in touch. This can be through phone calls, video calls, writing letters, or email. Ask both sets of parents or caregivers to set a date when you can visit. Knowing that you have a plan to see each other again will give you something to look forward to.

Plan a special farewell party. This can be just for the two of you or all your family and friends. Make something for each other as a memory gift. This could be a photo with a frame you have made yourself.

Make a memory box for each other. Include drawings or photos of your favorite places to visit. Add a memory of the fun things you do together.

Changing schools

Changing schools can be hard. You have to leave behind your friends, the routine you know, and the teachers you like.

Planning a school move will help you feel less nervous about the big change.

If you feel scared, sad, or anxious about the school move, talk to someone about it. Draw or write a list of the things that are worrying you.

Think of the good things about going to a new school, such as making new friends and trying new activities. If you have positive thoughts about the change, it will make it less scary.

See if you can visit your new school before you start. Get to know where your classroom is and where the washrooms are. Ask where you can hang your coat. Knowing these things will make you feel in control and less stressed.

Saying good-bye

It can be sad if your teacher leaves. Saying good-bye to someone you like very much is one of the hardest things to do. Learning how to cope with changes will help you to look forward to the future.

Throughout life we will have to say good-bye to people. It is OK to be sad and to miss them.

The best way to build resilience is to have many good memories. You could make a good-bye card for your teacher. Write a poem inside it to say why the teacher was special.

Suggest to the class that you get together and make the teacher a scrapbook as a reminder of the class. Plan what you will put in the scrapbook. What was the best thing your teacher taught you? What did you do that was the most fun?

Be resilient!

Being resilient means being able to cope with times when you feel sad or are going through a situation that makes you feel afraid or anxious. Here is a reminder of how accepting change is a great way to help you become resilient.

- Accepting change means you look forward to trying new things instead of being scared of them. Accepting change makes you more **flexible**. This means you do not get so upset or stressed when changes happen.

- When change is making you feel anxious, talk to someone about it. Talking is a great way to help you bounce back from those worries.

- Practice making changes every day so you get used to them. You could try a different routine when you get up. Take a different route to school or eat a new food.

- When you play games with your friends, take turns changing the rules. This gets you used to thinking and behaving differently.

- Do some exercise when change makes you feel anxious. Try dancing to your favorite music, playing a sport, or skipping. Exercise will help you cope.

Notes for parents, caregivers, and teachers

It is perfectly natural for children to be nervous about change. To build resilience you need to encourage a positive attitude toward change.

When a change is coming up, talk to the child about it. Keep calm and upbeat about the change.

Don't dismiss the child's anxiety as silly, stupid, or nothing to worry about. Talk about how the child is feeling. Then try to put a positive spin on the change. Think of interesting and fun things that could happen as a result of the change.

At home, involve the child in the change. For example, let them help with packing or choosing new school things. If you are moving to a new home or school, explore the area together before the move takes place. See if the child can visit their new school before they start.

Children who feel safe and secure are more likely to deal with change successfully. Reassure your child that whatever happens, you are there to love and support them.

In the classroom, watch out for new students who seem withdrawn. This could be a sign that they are not coping with change. Talk to them to find out what their worries are.

Have classroom talks about change and what it means to students. Encourage them to draw pictures or write poems and stories about how they feel about change.

At home or school, read through this book together. Talk about each scenario. Do some role-playing exercises based on the scenarios. Encourage the child to think of positive and fun things about change.

Glossary

anxious Feeling worried or nervous about how something is going to turn out

disappointed Feeling let down by something you expected

emotions Feelings such as happy, sad, and angry

flexible Able to change and do something differently

jealous Feeling envy, such as when someone has something that you want

positive Feeling happy about something

reframing Looking at something in a different way

routine Doing something in the same order every time you do it

secure Safe

self-confidence Trusting in your own abilities

Websites and helplines

If you need advice or someone to talk to, visit these websites or try these helplines.

www.boystown.org is an organization that helps children and youth in the United States. It has a helpline that has trained English and Spanish counselors working 24 hours a day, every day of the year. Call 1-800-448-3000.

www.kidshelpphone.ca has helpful information for children and youth in Canada. It has a helpline with trained English and French counselors. Call 1-800-668-6868.

www.mindyourmind.ca is a helpful website that gives tips on coping with issues and how to ask people for help.

Index